STAY SAFE. BE WISE.

By Tiffanie Danielle

A conversation starter to educate children about trafficking and other important topics.

This book is dedicated to the incredible staff and students at Become Pvt Ltd in Kathmandu, Nepal.
Your passion, resilience, and dedication encourage hope and change.
May you continue to grow, learn, and inspire.

FREE pdf Workbook

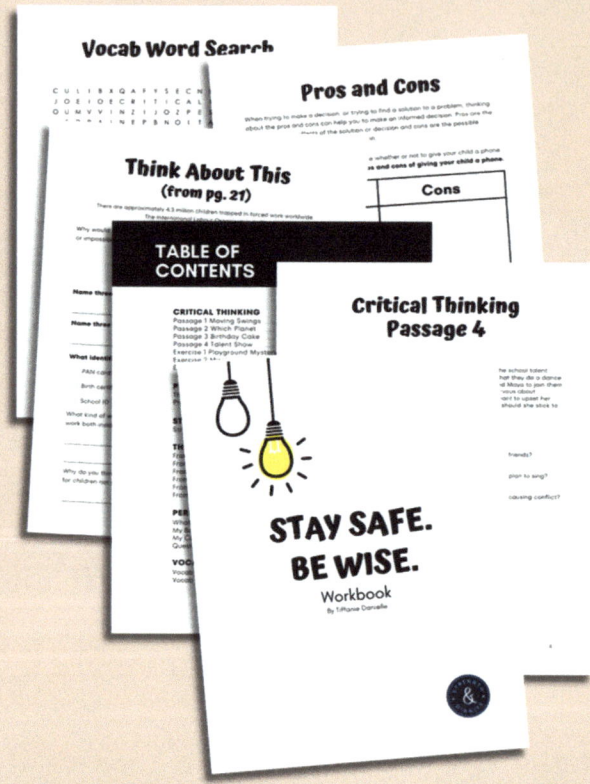

at www.strengthanddignity.net/freebies

A Note From the Author

Dear Parents, Guardians, Educators and Caregivers,

This book is intended to be used as a resource that I believe will be instrumental in fostering important conversations with children. This book introduces critical topics such as human trafficking, personal safety, and making informed decisions. I firmly believe that raising awareness and educating youth about these topics at an early age is essential not only for their safety but also for combating these evils in the world.

Throughout the light-hearted rhymes in this book, you'll find vocabulary words highlighted in yellow, along with relevant statistics and critical thinking questions, all of which are designed to facilitate conversation and further exploration. Definitions for each vocabulary word can be found at the back of this book.

Be sure to go to www.strengthanddignity.net/freebies to download the accompanying FREE pdf workbook.

Tiffanie Danielle

Highlighted words can be found in the Vocab list at the end of this book.

Critical Thinking

helps us to question and helps us to see...
What is true, what is false, what is meant to be.

Critical thinking helps us to make wise decisions.

Critical Thinking Questions

- What is happening?
- Why is it important?
- What is the source?
- Who is the information for?
- Who or what will it affect?
- What is the cost?
- What is needed?
- How long will it take?
- How do I know?
- What else matters?

Some problems are

BiG,

some problems
are small...

These 5 steps can help to solve them all.

1. **Define** the problem
2. Gather information
3. **Brainstorm** solutions
4. Decide and **implement**
5. **Evaluate** and **refine**

Just like exercising helps muscles grow, practicing problem solving helps your brain get stronger.

Problem Solving Skills...

- Improve the ability to make wise decisions

- Boost confidence

- Increase creativity

- Lead to better teamwork and relationships

- Improve the ability to handle hard situations

Children need a
place to grow...
Where love and
safety overflow.

Where can you go if you're scared or sad... Or when somebody makes you feel bad?

Who in your life

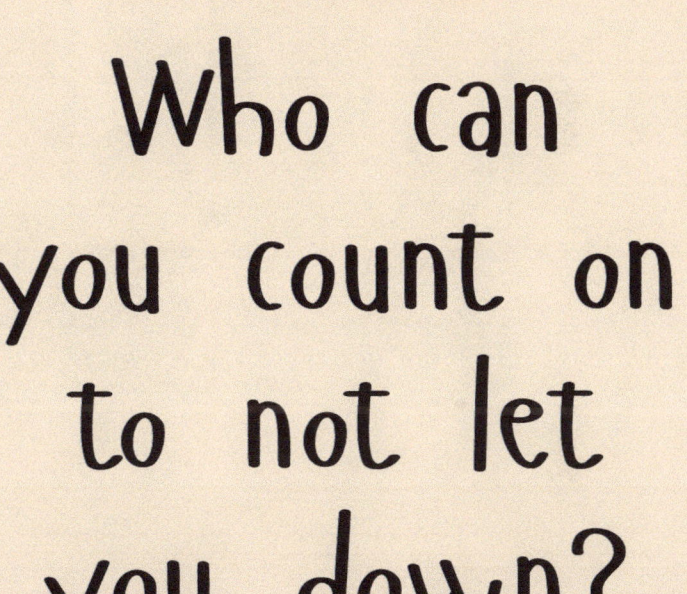

is safe and sound?

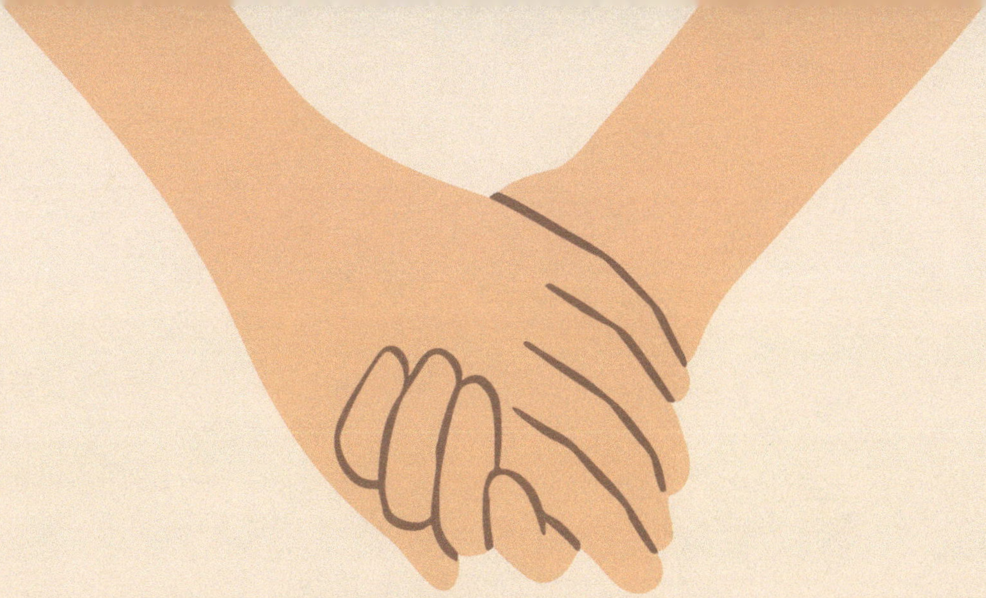

Who can you count on to not let you down?

If a stranger comes your way, while you are outside to play... Stay nearby to those you trust, and call for help when you must.

Never leave with a stranger... It could lead you into danger.

If a stranger
talks to you online...
Meeting in-person
is never fine.

If someone offers you
money or fame...
It's almost always their own
interests they aim to gain.

Globally, around 1.2 million children per year are ==abducted== or ==coerced== into ==exploitation.==

The International Labour Organization (ILO)

Think About This

Nowadays, many ==victims== are ==groomed== online.

Why can it be easy for a bad person to trick a child online?
Do you think it is difficult or easy to coerce people into doing wrong things for money?
Why or why not?

Not everything is for everyone to hear and see... You must always ask "what is good and healthy for me?"

If someone shows you or you find, something <mark>inappropriate</mark> for your eyes...
Turn it off,
look away,
and tell an adult
without delay.

12 percent of all internet sites include some form of inappropriate content.

The Internet Watch Foundation (IWF)

Think About This

It is important to be cautious when navigating the internet.

The internet holds a lot of inappropriate photos, stories, videos, gif's, jokes etc. Why is it important to avoid such content?

It's illegal for anyone to seek...

Your identification documents to keep.

Taking a minor from their family's care...

is rarely good, no matter where.

When kids are taken far from home...

It could be to a bad place where they feel all alone.

Kids are meant to learn and play... and should not be forced to work all day.

FACT-CHECKED

There are approximately 4.3 million children trapped in forced work worldwide.

The International Labour Organization (ILO)

Think About This

Many victims of ==trafficking== and exploitation have their passports and identity documents taken and kept by the bad people who trafficked or exploited them.

Why would this make it difficult or impossible for them to leave or to get help?

If anyone asks you
to do a job...

But keeps all the money
you earned, it's wrong.

When adults have jobs, it's important to know...

What a ==living wage== is, so that families can live and grow.

Globally, about 327 million workers earn less than a living wage.

International Labour Organization (ILO)

Think About This

When workers don't earn a living wage it means that they don't make enough money to cover their basic needs.

Why would an employer pay less than living wages?

It's illegal for minors to marry...

Marriage is for grownups, and consent is necessary.

Approximately 12 million girls are married before the age of 18 each year.

United Nations Children's Fund (UNICEF)

Think About This

Child marriage can have a significant impact on the education, health, and overall wellbeing of girls.

How could these things be impacted by child marriage? How/why do you think childhood marriage happens?

Your body is yours,
and that's for sure...

You should never feel
unsafe or unsure.

Kids should only be touched in healthy ways...

And <mark>abuse</mark> must be reported always.

Hundreds of millions of children globally have experienced abuse.

World Health Organization (WHO)

Think About This

Many children do not know the difference between good and bad touches. And many ==offenders== tell children not to tell anyone when they touch them.

What are good touches? What are bad touches? Who should you talk to if someone is touching you in ways that make you feel bad or unsure?

Use your voice when you need...

speaking up is good indeed.

It's important
to learn
when and
how to say
no...
And to know
when it is
time to go.

When others
push
and tell you
to try...

It's okay to
question
and ask why.

32

Questions to Ask

Will this break any rules, restrictions, or ==boundaries==?

Could this harm me or anyone else?

Is this ==beneficial==? How?

Would I have to lie?

What are the ==consequences==?

Think About This

It's important to choose good friends who won't ==peer pressure== you into doing things you shouldn't.

Why would someone choose to hang out with friends who do bad things? What kinds of things make a good friend?

Stand your ground and do not do...
Anything that you do not want to.

Healthy Boundaries

Personal Space
You have the right to say "no" if someone is too close or touches you in any way that makes you feel unsafe or unsure.

Secrets
Good secrets are about things like surprise birthday parties. Bad secrets make you feel uncomfortable, threatened, or scared. Bad secrets should always be told to an adult.

Online Safety
Limiting your time online, not communicating with strangers, having filters and parental controls set, not having access to the internet at night, and limiting (or avoiding) social media will all help keep you safe.

Stranger Danger

Do not accept gifts, rides, or favors from strangers, and tell an adult you trust when a stranger approaches you inappropriately.

Body Parts

Private parts are private and should never be touched or looked at except in specific situations, like a doctor's visit with a parent/guardian present.

Safe Words

Establish a "safe word" that only trusted adults know in case someone ever needs to pick you up suddenly or unexpectedly.

Public Safety

It is important to know where to find safe people and safe public places to go in the case of an emergency or if you get lost.

Friends and Peers

Not all friends live in safe homes and some friends may choose to do things that are wrong or unsafe. It is not always safe to have sleepovers and you should never go anywhere with a friend without permission from your parent/guardian. It is okay for you to say "no" to your friends. Sometimes it is okay to not share everything you have or everything you know with friends. It is okay to have a different opinion from your friends and it is okay to not agree with everything your friends do, say or believe.

Privacy

It is not safe to give personal information, such as your full name, address, email, phone number, school or information about your family to strangers on-line or in-person. It is also unsafe to send personal documents or pictures of yourself to people online.

Priorities
Family time, school and rest are all important and anything that takes away from these things should be limited.

Words
You do not have to listen to or accept unkind words, teasing, or bullying. Talk to a trusted adult if someone is being mean or hurtful.

Choosing right is never wrong...

You are brave and can stand up strong.

Questions to Ask

How can I say "no" respectfully?

What could I/we do instead?

Where is a safe place I can go?

Who should I tell?

Think About This

It's easier to say no and walk away from something that doesn't feel right when you already know your boundaries.

What could happen that you might need to speak up about? What are things you might need to say no to when hanging out with friends?

Now you know how to stay safe and be wise.... So act smart, stay alert, and don't **compromise**.

Vocab

Critical Thinking: To carefully think about something to figure out what is right or true, or what makes sense.

Define: To identify and then describe or explain a word, idea, etc.

Brainstorm: Thinking of as many ideas as you can about something, even if they seem silly, bad, or unhelpful.

Implement: To take an idea or a plan and actually do it. To put something into action.

Evaluate: To look at something carefully to see how good or bad it is or how well it does or doesn't work.

Refine: To make something better or to improve it.

Inappropriate: Something that isn't right or okay for the situation, like words, pictures, or actions that can make people feel embarrassed, uncomfortable, or upset.

Victim: Someone who has been hurt or treated badly by someone else. A victim is the person or child who has been abused, trafficked, exploited etc.

Grooming: When someone is friendly or nice to a child to make the child feel special or important, or to make the child trust them so that they can trick the child into doing things that are bad, unsafe, or wrong.

Abduction: When a person or child is taken away from where they are supposed to be without permission.

Coerced: When someone forces a person or child to do something they don't want to do by threatening, scaring, tricking them, etc.

Exploitation: When someone is using another person or child unfairly to get something they want without caring about how it might hurt the person or child.

Minor: A person who is legally still considered a child or teenager; someone who is not yet an adult.

Consent: Giving permission for something to happen without feeling pressured or forced.

Trafficking: When someone abducts or tricks people or children to go and be used for bad things, like making them work with little or no pay while treating them badly.

Living Wage: The amount of money a person needs to earn to cover basic family needs like food, a home, and clothes.

Abuse: When someone hurts another person or child on purpose or treats them very badly. It can be physical or emotional and it makes the person or child feel sad, scared, or unsafe.

Offender: Someone who does something wrong or bad, or who breaks the rules.

Peer Pressure: When someone feels like they have to do something because friends or others are doing it or expecting them to do it.

Boundaries: The rules or limits set to keep a person or child safe and comfortable.

Beneficial: When something is good for you or helps you in a positive way.

Consequences: The effects or results of something you do. They can be good or bad.

Priorities: The things that are most important to you and need to be done first before other things.

Compromise: When someone gives up some of what they want in order to agree on something that works for everyone, or in order to make others happy.

Download the **FREE** pdf workbook at
www.strengthanddignity.net